Reflections on the Life of the Spirit

Ruhi Institute

Books in the Series:

Below are the current titles in the series designed by the Ruhi Institute. The books are intended to be used as the main sequence of courses in a systematic effort to enhance the capacity of youth and adults to serve their communities. The Ruhi Institute is also developing a set of courses that branch out from the third book in the series for training Bahá'í children's class teachers, as well as another set from Book 5 for raising up animators of junior youth groups. These, too, are indicated in the list below. It should be noted that the list may undergo change as experience in the field advances, and additional titles will be added as a number of curricular elements under development reach the stage where they can be made widely available.

Book 1   *Reflections on the Life of the Spirit*

Book 2   *Arising to Serve*

Book 3   *Teaching Children's Classes, Grade 1*

          Teaching Children's Classes, Grade 2 (branch course)

          Teaching Children's Classes, Grade 3 (branch course)

          Teaching Children's Classes, Grade 4 (branch course)

Book 4   *The Twin Manifestations*

Book 5   *Releasing the Powers of Junior Youth*

          Initial Impulse: The first branch course of Book 5

          Widening Circle: The second branch course of Book 5

Book 6   *Teaching the Cause*

Book 7   *Walking Together on a Path of Service*

Book 8   *The Covenant of Bahá'u'lláh*

Book 9   *Gaining an Historical Perspective*

Book 10   *Building Vibrant Communities*

Book 11   *Material Means*

Book 12   (forthcoming)

Book 13   *Engaging in Social Action*

Book 14   (forthcoming)

Ruhi Institute
Cali, Colombia
Email: instituto@ruhi.org
Website: www.ruhi.org

Contents

A Few Thoughts for the Tutor

The number of localities in which *Reflections on the Life of the Spirit*, the first book of the main sequence of courses offered by the Ruhi Institute, is studied throughout the world has been on the rise for many years. In the vast majority of cases, the material is read and discussed by a group of friends, who may constitute a study circle that meets regularly, may come together in a campaign arranged for intensive study, or may gather in a camp during school holidays. Whatever the occasion, one member of the group acts as a tutor. The relationship between the tutor and the other participants is not one of teacher-to-student; all are consciously engaged in a process in which everyone is seeking to learn. But the tutor is not a detached and passive facilitator of discussion either. Having completed a sufficient number of courses in the sequence and undertaken the acts of service they encourage, he or she is able to assist every member of the group in achieving the purpose of the material being studied. Those who act as a tutor of Book 1 may find it helpful to review the ideas presented in this introduction from time to time.

Participants worldwide come to this first institute course from diverse backgrounds. Some are already members of the Bahá'í community who hope to enhance their capacity to serve the Cause they have embraced. Others see the course as the beginning of their investigation of the Bahá'í Faith as a religion. Still others are attracted to Bahá'í ideals and wish to acquaint themselves with the community's aims and endeavors. And there are an increasing number of young people in particular who, wanting to develop their capacity to serve society, often through one or another program promoted by the Bahá'í community, take the course as an initial step.

From the outset, it should be clear to every participant that the courses of the Ruhi Institute trace a path of service to humanity, upon which we each walk at our own pace, assisting and being assisted by others. Treading this path implies the pursuit of a twofold moral purpose: to attend to one's own spiritual and intellectual growth and to contribute to the transformation of society. Progress on the path entails the development of a number of capabilities that require understanding and knowledge, spiritual qualities and praiseworthy attitudes, as well as a host of abilities and skills. The sources of knowledge upon which the books of the Institute draw are, on the one hand, the teachings of the Bahá'í Faith and, on the other, the accumulating experience of the worldwide Bahá'í community in furthering material and spiritual civilization. It is Bahá'u'lláh's vision of the individual we can become and of the civilization we can build that inspires the Institute. It is assumed that all participants, independent of background, are open to embracing this vision, which is explicit in every unit of every book.

In a world where creeds and ideologies are willing to employ any means possible to win adherents, someone unfamiliar with the Faith may have genuine questions about the intentions of the Ruhi Institute, most notably, "Am I being asked to change my religion?" or "Am I being asked to join a religion?" Such questions offer the tutor a chance to explain the purpose of the sequence of courses as outlined above. While it is natural that Bahá'ís would be eager to see their friends join the community, their own teachings prohibit them, a tutor may wish to add, from engaging in proselytization. Walking the path of service opened up by the institute courses calls for an ever-deepening understanding of Bahá'u'lláh's teachings, which the materials endeavor to set forth unequivocally; acceptance and faith are matters to be contemplated by each individual freely and without pressure.

Not surprisingly, then, it is with the question of understanding, so central to all the books in the sequence, that this first one begins. To read from the Holy Writings is not the same as reading the many thousands of pages that a person sees in a lifetime, and the unit, "Understanding the Bahá'í Writings", seeks to foster the habit of reading passages from the Sacred Text every day and meditating on their meaning, a habit that will greatly aid participants as they embark on the path of service. To guide them in its study, the tutor must give a great deal of thought to the subject of understanding.

The Bahá'í Writings contain profound spiritual truths, and even as we strive to advance in our understanding of their infinite meaning, we know that we can never reach a definitive end. We generally gain a basic comprehension of the immediate meaning of a passage when reading it for the first time, and Section 1 of the unit takes this as a starting point. Thus, after reading the quotation, "The betterment of the world can be accomplished through pure and goodly deeds, through commendable and seemly conduct", participants are simply asked, "How can the betterment of the world be accomplished?" At a glance, most of the questions and exercises of this kind appear to be too simple. But years of experience seem to justify the Institute's decision to begin this way. We all need to be reminded that, in its haste to find the layers of truth in a passage, the mind should not overlook its obvious meaning. Attention to this first level of comprehension also proves vital to group consultation; it strengthens unity of thought, readily attainable when personal opinions are allowed to be illumined by Divine wisdom.

It is important to note here that understanding the immediate meaning of most passages does not benefit from a long discussion of single words out of context. That said, it may be necessary, on occasion, for a group to look up a word in the dictionary. What may be more fruitful, however, is for the participants to learn how to infer the meanings of words from whole sentences and paragraphs.

For understanding to expand beyond the realm of immediate meaning, examples that show how ideas find concrete expression can be helpful. All that is called for in this respect are straightforward exercises. In Section 2, for instance, participants are asked to determine, in light of a passage they have just read, whether certain characteristics are commendable. In a similar exercise in Section 4, they are encouraged to name five virtues and then decide whether it is possible to acquire any of them in the absence of truthfulness—described in the Writings as "the foundation of all human virtues".

To achieve its purpose, the unit demands a further advance in understanding by challenging participants to think about some of the implications of the passages presented. In Section 2, they are required to determine whether the statement "There are so few good people in the world that their actions do not have any effect" is true. Here the intent is not to elicit mere opinion. The tutor must pause and query the reason for the participants' answers. That the statement must necessarily be false because it contradicts the first quotation in the preceding section is the conclusion to which the group should come. The question of whether Bahá'ís may confess their sins to others is also an example of this kind of exercise. It refers to the prohibition in the teachings against confession as a means of absolving sin, which, not mentioned expressly in any of the passages studied, can be drawn out by exploring the meaning of the verse, "Bring thyself to account each day ere thou art summoned to a reckoning."

By no means do the exercises in the unit attempt to encompass the range of meaning enshrined in the passages under consideration. One question every tutor must contemplate is how much discussion should go into any given exercise. Here it is important to bear in mind that prolonging deliberations by introducing many related but peripheral concepts tends to diminish the effectiveness of the material. Every group needs to establish a reasonable rhythm of progress; participants should feel a distinct sense that they are advancing steadily according to their own possibilities. The tutor must, however, stay attentive, lest sections are passed over quickly and superficially without the thoughtful analysis of exercises; groups that have proceeded in this way, merely filling in answers, have never attained lasting results.

One final point deserves some mention: It falls on the tutor to ensure that every member of the group remains engaged in the process of learning fostered by the material. To elicit participation without pressuring any individual to speak is often the challenge. What should be realized from the start is that this challenge is seldom met by asking questions such as, "What does this mean to you?" Questions of this kind tend to reduce knowledge and truth to the level of opinion. And it then proves difficult to create an atmosphere in which consultation among the members of the group actually gives rise to increased understanding.

The second unit in the book is concerned, like the first, with a habit essential to spiritual life: praying regularly. It makes explicit in the opening section the concept of "path of service", suggesting that, to walk this path, we must be imbued with a twofold purpose. Participants examine an initial set of quotations that offer insight into the nature of this purpose, a theme that will be elaborated in future courses.

Against the backdrop of this theme the unit takes up its exploration of the significance of prayer. It adopts an approach similar to the one described in the preceding paragraphs. Questions and exercises are formulated so as to advance understanding of the meaning of passages from the Writings being studied. As the group progresses through the unit, the tutor may be required to dissipate doubts by analyzing notions rooted in interpretations and practices of the past. In some traditions, ritual and form have gradually overshadowed the importance of inner state, and so many ignore the necessity of prayer, which, for the human soul, is no less crucial than is food in nourishing the body.

Above all, then, the unit aspires to awaken in participants the desire to "converse with God" and to draw near to Him. Among the ideas addressed are what it means to enter into a state of prayer, the posture of our hearts and minds when we do so, and the conditions that should be created in our surroundings, whether we are alone or in a gathering. Indeed, after giving some thought to the forces generated through communal worship, participants are asked to consider hosting a gathering for prayer and devotions.

The study of the third unit of the book, "Life and Death", will strengthen, it is hoped, commitment to walking the path of service and endow it with more profound meaning. Service in this world is best understood in the fullest context of life, which extends beyond our earthly existence and continues forever as our souls progress throughout the worlds of God. In a process of education, as opposed to technical training, participants should become increasingly conscious of the meaning and significance of what they are doing. Only if such consciousness grows, experience indicates, will they come to see themselves as active, responsible "owners" of their own learning.

Each section of the unit opens with one to three quotations from the Bahá'í Writings, followed by a few exercises. The language of the passages quoted in this unit is more demanding than in the previous two. There is no need, of course, for the group to dwell on difficult words; the tutor will want to ensure that everyone grasps the central idea addressed in each section, which is precisely what the exercises try to bring out.

Given the nature of the subject, exercises involving concrete examples are few and far between. Most tend to operate at a conceptual level. What should be noted is that some of the questions posed by the exercises cannot be answered quickly or in a clear-cut way. They are introduced to raise awareness about the subject; if participants merely think about such questions, the objective of learning will have been fulfilled.

The first several sections focus on the relationship between the soul and the body, which, together, constitute the human being in this plane of existence. The central idea presented in these sections is that the soul is not a physical entity; its association with the body can be likened to the light that appears in a mirror. Neither the dust covering its surface nor the eventual destruction of the mirror can affect the splendor of the light itself. Death is just a change of condition, when the association between the body and soul is broken; afterwards, the soul progresses eternally towards its Creator.

The unit turns next to the question of the purpose of life—to know God and to attain His presence. Discussion here revolves around two broad themes. The first is the purpose of our lives in this world, and the second the journey of the soul after death. The soul is a sign of God and can reflect all of His names and attributes. Yet the potential within the human being is latent; it can only be developed with the help of the Manifestations of God, those sanctified Beings Who come from time to time to guide humanity. Through the spiritual education They provide, the treasures hidden within us can be revealed.

As for the journey of the soul after death, a series of ideas are laid out for participants to contemplate: that those faithful to God will attain unto true happiness; that none of us can ever know our own end and, therefore, we should forgive one another and not feel superior to others; that in the next world, as in this one, the soul will continue to progress and the spiritual faculties we developed here will aid and assist us there; that we will recognize our loved ones in the realms beyond, will remember our lives in this world, and will enjoy companionship with holy and sanctified souls.

The unit comes to a close with a passage from the Writings of Bahá'u'lláh in which we are assured of the benefits of the next world and urged not to allow the changes and chances of this life to bring us sorrow. Participants are asked to reflect, then, on the implications of what they have studied for their own lives.

Understanding the Bahá'í Writings

Purpose

To strengthen the habit of reading passages
from the Holy Writings every day
and reflecting on their meaning

SECTION 1

The purpose of this unit is to assist you in developing and strengthening the habit of reading passages from the Holy Writings every day and reflecting on their meaning. The unit begins with a simple exercise that asks you to read a one-sentence statement from the Writings and respond to a question, the answer to which is the statement itself. Though easy to carry out, the exercise will help you to reflect on the meaning of the statements cited and to memorize them.

"The betterment of the world can be accomplished through pure and goodly deeds, through commendable and seemly conduct."[1]

1.   How can the betterment of the world be accomplished? _____

   _____

   _____

"Beware, O people of Bahá, lest ye walk in the ways of them whose words differ from their deeds."[2]

2.   In whose ways should we not walk? _____

   _____

   _____

"O Son of Being! Bring thyself to account each day ere thou art summoned to a reckoning . . ."[3]

3.   What should we do before we are summoned to a reckoning?_____

   _____

   _____

"Say: O brethren! Let deeds, not words, be your adorning."[4]

4.   What should be our true adorning? _____

   _____

"Holy words and pure and goodly deeds ascend unto the heaven of celestial glory."[5]

5.   What do holy words and pure and goodly deeds do? _____

   _____

   _____

SECTION 2

Below are a number of exercises related to the quotations you have just read. They are intended to help you reflect further on the significance of the passages in your group and should not be done mechanically. This does not mean that every exercise requires a great deal of discussion. When the exercise is challenging, however, the tutor of your group will assist you in exploring it thoroughly.

1. When something is "commendable", it is worthy of praise. Which of the following are commendable?

   _____ To be a good worker

   _____ To respect others

   _____ To be studious

   _____ To be a liar

   _____ To be lazy

   _____ To serve others

2. What does the phrase "ere thou art summoned to a reckoning" mean? _____
   _____

3. Which of the following statements are true?

   _____ There are so few good people in the world that their actions do not have any effect.

   _____ Something is correct when it is in agreement with the opinions of other people.

   _____ Something is correct when it is in agreement with the teachings of God.

4. Which of the following are pure and goodly deeds?

   _____ Taking care of and teaching children

   _____ Stealing

   _____ Praying for the progress of others

   _____ Telling a small lie to get out of trouble

   _____ Helping others and expecting a reward

5. In which of the following situations do the words of the person differ from his or her deeds?

   _____ Someone keeps repeating that we should all be united but behaves in a way that creates conflict.

   _____ Someone praises the value of a chaste life but has sexual relations outside of marriage.

_____ Someone consumes alcohol occasionally, while professing to follow a religious faith that prohibits drinking.

Someone advocates the equality of men and women but, as an employer, pays women less than men for the same job.

6. Is it permissible for a Bahá'í to confess to another person? _____

7. What should he or she do instead of confessing? _____
    _____

8. What does the phrase "the heaven of celestial glory" mean? _____
    _____

9. What effect do bad deeds have on the world? _____
    _____

10. What effect do bad deeds have on those who commit them? _____
    _____

SECTION 3

Now read and reflect on the following quotations from the Writings. Then try to memorize them.

"Truthfulness is the foundation of all human virtues."[6]

1. What is the foundation of all human virtues? _____
    _____

"Without truthfulness progress and success, in all the worlds of God, are impossible for any soul."[7]

2. What is impossible without truthfulness? _____
    _____

"Beautify your tongues, O people, with truthfulness, and adorn your souls with the ornament of honesty."[8]

3. With what should we beautify our tongues? _____
    _____

4.   With what should we adorn our souls? _____

_____

"Let your eye be chaste, your hand faithful, your tongue truthful and your heart enlightened."[9]

5.   How should our eye be? _____ Our hand? _____

Our tongue? _____ Our heart? _____

"They who dwell within the tabernacle of God, and are established upon the seats of everlasting glory, will refuse, though they be dying of hunger, to stretch their hands and seize unlawfully the property of their neighbor, however vile and worthless he may be."[10]

6.   What should we refuse to do even if we are dying of hunger? _____

_____

_____

SECTION 4

As you probably noted in Section 2, some of the exercises in this unit call for definitive answers. In such cases, if there is doubt about the answer, the tutor of your group will be able to help you and your fellow participants reach unity of thought. For other exercises, it is the discussion itself that is valuable, and no one specific answer is expected. In the following, exercise 3 is of the first kind, while exercise 6 falls into the second category.

1.   Truthfulness is the foundation of all human virtues. List five virtues: _____

_____

_____

2.   Can we acquire these virtues without truthfulness? _____

3.   Which of the following statements are true?

_____ A person can be just even if he tells lies.

_____ Someone who steals has a faithful hand.

_____ A faithful hand never touches what does not belong to it.

_____ To look at pornographic material is contrary to Bahá'u'lláh's counsel to have an eye that is chaste.

_____ Truthfulness means not lying.

_____ Honesty is an ornament of the soul.

_____ A person who is not truthful can progress spiritually.

_____ It is all right to tell lies now and then.

_____ Stealing is acceptable before God if one is hungry.

_____ To take something without permission from its owner, thinking that we will return it later, is not stealing.

_____ When we act honestly and are fair and truthful, our heart is enlightened.

_____ It is impossible to make a business successful without cheating a little.

4. Is it possible to lie to oneself? _____

5. What do we lose when we tell a lie? _____

6. What would the world be like if we were all truthful and honest?_____

_____

_____

_____

SECTION 5

Read the following quotations and try to learn them by heart. Memorizing quotations from the Writings is highly rewarding, and you should exert your utmost to do so. Not everyone, of course, is able to memorize passages easily. Making the effort, however, helps us to engrave the ideas on our hearts and minds and to express them in words as close to the original text as possible.

"A kindly tongue is the lodestone of the hearts of men. It is the bread of the spirit, it clotheth the words with meaning, it is the fountain of the light of wisdom and understanding."[11]

1. How can a kindly tongue be described? _____

_____

_____

_____

2. What effect does a kindly tongue have on words? _____

_____

"O ye beloved of the Lord! In this sacred Dispensation, conflict and contention are in no wise permitted. Every aggressor deprives himself of God's grace."[12]

3. According to the above quotation, what is not permitted in this Dispensation? ___

_____

4. What does the aggressor do to himself? _____

_____

"Nothing whatever can, in this Day, inflict a greater harm upon this Cause than dissension and strife, contention, estrangement and apathy, among the loved ones of God."[13]

5. What conditions inflict the greatest harm on the Cause of God? _____

_____

_____

"Do not be content with showing friendship in words alone, let your heart burn with loving kindness for all who may cross your path."[14]

6. What kind of friendship should not satisfy us? _____

_____

7. What should burn brightly in our heart? _____

_____

"When a thought of war comes, oppose it by a stronger thought of peace. A thought of hatred must be destroyed by a more powerful thought of love."[15]

8. With what should a thought of war be opposed? _____

_____

9. With what should a thought of hate be destroyed? _____

_____

SECTION 6

With the above quotations in mind, carry out the following exercises:

1. "Lodestone" is another word for magnet. In what way does a kindly tongue act like a lodestone? _____

2. Which of the following statements proceed from a kindly tongue?

_____ "Don't bother me!"

_____ "Why don't you understand this?"

_____ "Would you care to wait, please?"

_____ "What terrible children!"

_____ "Thank you, you're very kind."

_____ "I don't have any time for you now. I'm busy."

3. In which of the following situations are conflict and contention present?

    _____ Two people express different ideas on some topic during consultation.

    _____ Two people become upset and argue with one another during consultation.

    _____ Two people stop attending a weekly devotional gathering because they are not on speaking terms with each other.

    _____ Members of a team collaborating on a project keep complaining, each one saying that the others are not doing their part.

4. Which of the following situations show signs of estrangement?

    _____ Two friends pass by one another on the street but ignore each other.

    _____ Someone arrives at a devotional gathering, and everyone greets her warmly.

    _____ Although they are polite to one another, two members of a group are reluctant to participate in a project together.

5. Decide whether the following statements are true:

    _____ One should say exactly what one thinks of others; it does not matter if their hearts are offended.

    _____ It is all right to tell lies to avoid conflict.

    _____ Conflict can be overcome with love and kindness.

    _____ Words are more effective when they are said with love.

    _____ It is all right to fight with someone if he starts it.

    _____ One has the right to be sharp with others when one is sick or sad.

    _____ It is unkind to laugh at others when they do something wrong.

    _____ When hard feelings exist between friends, each one should make a special effort to become closer to the other.

    _____ When hard feelings exist between friends, each one should wait until the other makes an effort to move closer.

SECTION 7

Read the quotations below and memorize them.

" . . . **backbiting quencheth the light of the heart, and extinguisheth the life of the soul.**"[16]

"Breathe not the sins of others so long as thou art thyself a sinner."[17]

"Speak no evil, that thou mayest not hear it spoken unto thee, and magnify not the faults of others that thine own faults may not appear great . . ."[18]

"O Son of Being! How couldst thou forget thine own faults and busy thyself with the faults of others?"[19]

1. What effect does backbiting have on the one who backbites? _____

   _____

2. What should we think of before breathing the sins of others? _____

   _____

3. What will happen to us if we magnify the faults of others? _____

   _____

4. What should we remember when we think of other people's faults? _____

   _____

SECTION 8

With the above quotations in mind, carry out the following exercises:

1. What happens to the progress of the soul of a person who focuses on other people's faults? _____

2. What effect does backbiting have on a community? _____

   _____

3. What do you do when a friend starts to talk about another person's faults? _____

   _____

4. Decide whether the following statements are true:

   _____ When we talk about someone's real faults, we are not backbiting.

   _____ When we talk about a person's praiseworthy qualities and his faults at the same time, we are not backbiting.

   _____ Backbiting has become a common practice in our society, and we should develop the discipline to avoid it.

   _____ If the listener promises not to repeat what we say about another person, there is no harm in backbiting.

_____ Backbiting is one of the greatest enemies of unity.

_____ If we acquire the habit of talking about other people all the time, we can easily fall into backbiting.

_____ When the capacities of different people are discussed in a Local Spiritual Assembly meeting in order to name the members of a committee, this is backbiting.

_____ When we feel the urge to backbite, we should remember our own faults.

_____ When we know a person is doing something that harms the Faith, we should discuss it with the members of the community.

_____ When we know a person is doing something that harms the Faith, we should only inform the Local Spiritual Assembly.

_____ It is not wrong for a married couple to talk about other people's faults since they should not keep secrets from each other.

SECTION 9

The purpose of this unit, as mentioned at the beginning, is to assist participants in their efforts to develop and strengthen the habit of reading passages from the Holy Writings every day and reflecting on their meaning. To read the verses of God every morning and evening is a teaching of Bahá'u'lláh conducive to our spiritual development. The following passage reminds us of the bounties we receive from fulfilling this obligation, and you are encouraged to commit it to memory:

"Immerse yourselves in the ocean of My words, that ye may unravel its secrets, and discover all the pearls of wisdom that lie hid in its depths."[20]

Having completed this unit, you may wish to acquire a book of Bahá'u'lláh's Writings and read from it every day. The Hidden Words is a good first choice.

REFERENCES

1. Bahá'u'lláh, cited by Shoghi Effendi, *The Advent of Divine Justice* (Wilmette: Bahá'í Publishing Trust, 2006, 2018 printing), par. 39, pp. 36–37.

2. *Gleanings from the Writings of Bahá'u'lláh* (Wilmette: Bahá'í Publishing Trust, 1983, 2017 printing), CXXXIX, par. 8, p. 345.

3. Bahá'u'lláh, *The Hidden Words* (Wilmette: Bahá'í Publishing Trust, 2003, 2012 printing), Arabic no. 31, p. 11.

4. Ibid., Persian no. 5, p. 24.

5. Ibid., Persian no. 69, p. 46.

6. 'Abdu'l-Bahá, cited by Shoghi Effendi, *The Advent of Divine Justice*, par. 40, p. 39.

7. Ibid.

8. *Gleanings from the Writings of Bahá'u'lláh*, CXXXVI, par. 6, p. 336.

9. *Tablets of Bahá'u'lláh Revealed after the Kitáb-i-Aqdas* (Wilmette: Bahá'í Publishing Trust, 1988, 2005 printing), no. 9.5, p. 138.

10. *Gleanings from the Writings of Bahá'u'lláh*, CXXXVII, par. 3, p. 338.

11. Ibid., CXXXII, par. 5, p. 327.

12. *Will and Testament of 'Abdu'l-Bahá* (Wilmette: Bahá'í Publishing Trust, 1944, 2013 printing), p. 26.

13. *Gleanings from the Writings of Bahá'u'lláh*, V, par. 5, p. 8.

14. From a talk given on 16 and 17 October 1911, published in *Paris Talks: Addresses Given by 'Abdu'l-Bahá in 1911* (Wilmette: Bahá'í Publishing, 2006, 2016 printing), no. 1.7, p. 6.

15. From a talk given by 'Abdu'l-Bahá on 21 October 1911, ibid., no. 6.7, p. 22.

16. *Gleanings from the Writings of Bahá'u'lláh*, CXXV, par. 3, p. 300.

17. *The Hidden Words*, Arabic no. 27, p. 10.

18. Ibid., Persian no. 44, p. 37.

19. Ibid., Arabic no. 26, p. 10.

20. *Gleanings from the Writings of Bahá'u'lláh*, LXX, par. 2, p. 154.

Prayer

Purpose

To reflect on the significance of prayer and
to reinforce the habit of praying regularly

SECTION 1

The courses of the Ruhi Institute are intended to help participants walk a path of service. We walk this path impelled by a twofold sense of purpose—to grow spiritually and intellectually and to contribute to the transformation of society. These two aspects of our purpose are inseparable from each other. Bahá'u'lláh exhorts us in one passage:

> **"Do not busy yourselves in your own concerns; let your thoughts be fixed upon that which will rehabilitate the fortunes of mankind and sanctify the hearts and souls of men."[1]**

In another passage, He makes clear:

> **" . . . the purpose for which mortal men have, from utter nothingness, stepped into the realm of being, is that they may work for the betterment of the world and live together in concord and harmony."[2]**

In relation to our inner condition, He declares:

> **"A pure heart is as a mirror; cleanse it with the burnish of love and severance from all save God, that the true sun may shine therein and the eternal morning dawn."[3]**

And 'Abdu'l-Bahá tells us:

> **"Your hearts must be pure and your intentions sincere in order that you may become recipients of the divine bestowals."[4]**

1. What should be the focus of our thoughts and concerns? _____

    _____

    _____

2. For what purpose have we stepped from utter nothingness into the realm of being?

    _____

    _____

    _____

3. With what should we cleanse the mirror of our heart? _____

    _____

4. What are some of the conditions that attract divine bestowals? _____

    _____

5.   Are any of the following true?

   –   First you should take care of yourself, and then you can take care of others.

   –   If you are always helping others, you will end up losing sight of your own goals.

   –   You are your closest friend.

   –   What is most important is finding out what makes you happy.

   –   Follow your dreams, and they will lead you to happiness.

   –   As long as you are not hurting anyone else, it does not matter what you do.

   –   It is all right for your motives to be selfish, as long as you do some good.

SECTION 2

A conviction central to our twofold purpose is that we have all been created noble. Bahá'u'lláh says:

> "O Son of Spirit! I created thee rich, why dost thou bring thyself down to poverty? Noble I made thee, wherewith dost thou abase thyself? Out of the essence of knowledge I gave thee being, why seekest thou enlightenment from anyone beside Me? Out of the clay of love I molded thee, how dost thou busy thyself with another? Turn thy sight unto thyself, that thou mayest find Me standing within thee, mighty, powerful and self-subsisting."[5]

Filling in the blanks below will help you reflect on this passage.

"O Son of Spirit! I created thee _____ , why dost thou bring thyself _____ to _____ ? _____ I _____ thee, wherewith dost thou _____ thyself? Out of the _____ of _____ I gave thee being, why _____ thou _____ from anyone beside _____ ? Out of the clay of _____ I _____ thee, how dost thou _____ thyself with _____ ? Turn thy _____ unto _____ , that thou mayest find _____ standing within thee, _____ , _____ and _____ _____ ."

To be true to the nobility of our souls, we must turn to the Source of our being and seek enlightenment from Him. One of the most compelling ways to achieve this is through prayer. Shoghi Effendi, Guardian of the Faith, tells us that its chief goal is "the development of the individual and society, through the acquisition of spiritual virtues and powers. It is the soul of man that has first to be fed. And this spiritual nourishment prayer can best provide."[6]

SECTION 3

God is the All-Knowing, the All-Wise. He created us and knows what is in our hearts and what is best for us. He does not need our prayers. Then why do we pray?

'Abdu'l-Bahá states:

"In the highest prayer, men pray only for the love of God, not because they fear Him or hell, or hope for bounty or heaven. . . . When a man falls in love with a human being, it is impossible for him to keep from mentioning the name of his beloved. How much more difficult is it to keep from mentioning the Name of God when one has come to love Him. . . . The spiritual man finds no delight in anything save in commemoration of God."[7]

And, in response to a query, He explains:

"If one friend loves another, is it not natural that he should wish to say so? Though he knows that that friend is aware of his love, does he still not wish to tell him of it? . . . It is true that God knows the wishes of all hearts; but the impulse to pray is a natural one, springing from man's love to God."[8]

1. Complete the following sentences:

   a. In the _____ prayer, we _____ only for the _____ of God, not because we fear Him or _____ , or hope for _____ or _____ .

   b. When we fall in _____ with another human being, it is _____ for us to keep from mentioning the _____ of our _____ . How much more _____ is it to keep from _____ the Name of _____ when one has come to _____ Him.

   c. A spiritual person finds _____ in nothing other than in _____ of God.

2. Why do we pray? _____

   _____

3. What does the phrase "commemoration of God" mean? _____

   _____

4. What is the most fervent wish of a person who loves another? _____

   _____

5. What does the impulse to pray spring from?_____

   _____

SECTION 4

In a prayer revealed by Bahá'u'lláh, we read:

"I beseech Thee . . . to make of my prayer a fire that will burn away the veils which have shut me out from Thy beauty, and a light that will lead me unto the ocean of Thy Presence."[9]

We ask of God in that same prayer:

"Make my prayer, O my Lord, a fountain of living waters whereby I may live as long as Thy sovereignty endureth, and may make mention of Thee in every world of Thy worlds."[10]

1.   In what sense can prayer be like a fire? What does it consume? _____

    _____

2.   Mention some veils that shut us out from God: _____

    _____

    _____

3.   Can prayer be like a light? Where does it lead us? _____

    _____

    _____

4.   Can prayer be like a fountain of living waters? What does it bestow upon our souls?

    _____

    _____

    _____

SECTION 5

Read and reflect on the following words of 'Abdu'l-Bahá:

"There is nothing sweeter in the world of existence than prayer. Man must live in a state of prayer. The most blessed condition is the condition of prayer and supplication. Prayer is conversation with God. The greatest attainment or the sweetest state is none other than conversation with God. It creates spirituality, creates mindfulness and celestial feelings, begets new attractions of the Kingdom and engenders the susceptibilities of the higher intelligence."[11]

1.   What is the sweetest state in the world of existence? _____

    _____

2.   What does the phrase "state of prayer" mean? _____

        _____

        _____

3.   Mention some of the attributes created by prayer: _____

        _____

        _____

4.   Review the quotations you have studied in these few sections and write five phrases
        on the nature of prayer.

        –   Prayer is _____

        –   Prayer is _____

        –   Prayer is _____

        –   Prayer is _____

        –   Prayer is _____

SECTION 6

Read the following words of Bahá'u'lláh and meditate on them:

"Intone, O My servant, the verses of God that have been received by thee, as intoned by them who have drawn nigh unto Him, that the sweetness of thy melody may kindle thine own soul, and attract the hearts of all men. Whoso reciteth, in the privacy of his chamber, the verses revealed by God, the scattering angels of the Almighty shall scatter abroad the fragrance of the words uttered by his mouth, and shall cause the heart of every righteous man to throb. Though he may, at first, remain unaware of its effect, yet the virtue of the grace vouchsafed unto him must needs sooner or later exercise its influence upon his soul. Thus have the mysteries of the Revelation of God been decreed by virtue of the Will of Him Who is the Source of power and wisdom."[12]

1.   What does the word "intone" mean? _____

        _____

2.   How should we intone the verses of God? _____

        _____

        _____

        _____

3.   What does the word "recite" mean? _____

_____

4.   What does the word "scatter" mean? _____

_____

5.   What effect will the sweetness of our melody have on our own souls? _____

_____

6.   What effect will the sweetness of our melody have on the hearts of others? _____

_____

_____

SECTION 7

You may wish to memorize the following two passages from a prayer revealed by Bahá'u'lláh:

"O God, my God! Look not upon my hopes and my doings, nay rather look upon Thy will that hath encompassed the heavens and the earth. By Thy Most Great Name, O Thou Lord of all nations! I have desired only what Thou didst desire, and love only what Thou dost love."[13]

"Too high art Thou for the praise of those who are nigh unto Thee to ascend unto the heaven of Thy nearness, or for the birds of the hearts of them who are devoted to Thee to attain to the door of Thy gate. I testify that Thou hast been sanctified above all attributes and holy above all names. No God is there but Thee, the Most Exalted, the All-Glorious."[14]

SECTION 8

'Abdu'l-Bahá states:

"It behooveth the servant to pray to and seek assistance from God, and to supplicate and implore His aid. Such becometh the rank of servitude, and the Lord will decree whatsoever He desireth, in accordance with His consummate wisdom."[15]

And He explains:

"Spirit has influence; prayer has spiritual effect. Therefore, we pray, 'O God! Heal this sick one!' Perchance God will answer. Does it matter who prays? God will answer the prayer of every servant if that prayer is urgent. His mercy is vast, illimitable. He answers the prayers of all His servants. He answers the prayer of this plant. The plant prays potentially, 'O God! Send me rain!' God answers the prayer, and the plant grows. God will answer anyone."[16]

It is natural that in our prayers we would ask God to fulfill our needs. Thus we pray for our health and the health of our loved ones, we pray for the spiritual and material progress of our families, and we pray for guidance. We ask for strength, for faith, and for confirmation in the path of service. In praying to God, we should, of course, remember that our goal in life is to align our will with His Will. Therefore, we must pray for His Will to be done and be ready to submit to it. If you commit the following words of 'Abdu'l-Bahá to memory, they will serve as a source of joy and assurance to you at all times:

> **"O thou who art turning thy face towards God! Close thine eyes to all things else, and open them to the realm of the All-Glorious. Ask whatsoever thou wishest of Him alone; seek whatsoever thou seekest from Him alone. With a look He granteth a hundred thousand hopes, with a glance He healeth a hundred thousand incurable ills, with a nod He layeth balm on every wound, with a glimpse He freeth the hearts from the shackles of grief. He doeth as He doeth, and what recourse have we? He carrieth out His Will, He ordaineth what He pleaseth. Then better for thee to bow down thy head in submission, and put thy trust in the All-Merciful Lord."[17]**

SECTION 9

From everything we have studied up to now, it is clear that turning to God in prayer is a vital requirement of a spiritual life. How especially sweet it is to pray to God soon after waking in the morning and at night before going to sleep. The time we spend praying each day and the number of prayers we say depend on our needs and our spiritual thirst. On every occasion, we are able to choose from the many prayers revealed by Bahá'u'lláh, the Báb, and 'Abdu'l-Bahá. Bahá'u'lláh has also revealed, however, three daily obligatory prayers. Shoghi Effendi says:

> **"The daily obligatory prayers are three in number. The shortest one consists of a single verse which has to be recited once every twenty-four hours at midday. The medium, which begins with the words, 'The Lord is witness that there is none other God but He,' has to be recited three times a day, in the morning, at noon and in the evening. This prayer is accompanied by certain physical acts and gestures. The long prayer, which is the most elaborate of the three, has to be recited only once in every twenty-four hours, and at any time one feels inclined to do so.**
>
> **"The believer is entirely free to choose any one of these three prayers, but is under the obligation of reciting one of them, and in accordance with any specific directions with which it may be accompanied."[18]**

And he continues:

> **"These daily obligatory prayers, together with a few other specific ones, such as the Healing Prayer, the Tablet of Aḥmad, have been invested by Bahá'u'lláh with a special potency and significance, and should therefore be accepted as such and be recited by the believers with unquestioning faith and confidence, that through them they may enter into a much closer communion with God, and identify themselves more fully with His laws and precepts."[19]**

The three obligatory prayers revealed by Bahá'u'lláh are said individually. The kind of congregational prayer where a daily obligatory prayer is recited in a group according to a certain ritual does not exist in the Bahá'í Faith. The Prayer for the Dead is the only congregational prayer prescribed by Bahá'í law. It is to be recited before interment by one of those present, while the remainder of the group stands in silence.

1.   What does the word "obligatory" mean?_____

_____

2.   How many daily obligatory prayers has Bahá'u'lláh revealed? _____

_____

3.   Should we recite all three prayers every day?_____

4.   If we choose to say the Long Obligatory Prayer, how many times should we recite it each day? _____

5.   How many times, if we choose to say the Medium Obligatory Prayer? _____

6.   How many times, if we choose the Short Obligatory Prayer? _____

7.   Mention some of the prayers which have a special power: _____

_____

_____

8.   Memorize, if you have not already done so, the Short Obligatory Prayer:

"I bear witness, O my God, that Thou hast created me to know Thee and to worship Thee. I testify, at this moment, to my powerlessness and to Thy might, to my poverty and to Thy wealth.

"There is none other God but Thee, the Help in Peril, the Self-Subsisting."[20]

9.   To what do we attest in this prayer? _____

_____

_____

_____

SECTION 10

We should remember that, in addition to the blessings we receive from obeying the law of obligatory prayer and the nourishment we obtain from saying other prayers individually, our souls are uplifted when we hear prayers being recited in gatherings, large or small. Bahá'u'lláh tells us:

"Gather ye together with the utmost joy and fellowship and recite the verses revealed by the merciful Lord. By so doing the doors of true knowledge will be opened to your inner beings, and ye will then feel your souls endowed with steadfastness and your hearts filled with radiant joy."[21]

We all derive great joy from the knowledge that, around the world, devotional gatherings in which friends and neighbors come together to commune with God are multiplying by the thousands. The Universal House of Justice writes:

"Devotional meetings are occasions where any soul may enter, inhale the heavenly fragrances, experience the sweetness of prayer, meditate upon the Creative Word, be transported on the wings of the spirit, and commune with the one Beloved. Feelings of fellowship and common cause are generated, particularly in the spiritually heightened conversations that naturally occur at such times and through which the 'city of the human heart' may be opened."[22]

When we feel moved to pray, we wait quietly for a moment in order to cleanse our minds of the things of this world. While praying, we keep our thoughts centered on God. After we have recited prayers, we remain silent for some time and do not move abruptly into another activity. The same is true when we listen to prayers offered by others in a gathering. On such occasions, we maintain a prayerful attitude and follow the words closely, as though we were the one reciting them.

1. With what spirit should we gather together when reciting the verses of God? _____

    _____

2. What will be the effect of our gathering together to recite the verses of God? _____

    _____

    _____

    _____

3. Devotional meetings are occasions where any soul can

    — _____ ,

    — _____ ,

    — _____ ,

    — _____ ,

    — _____ , and

    — _____ .

4. What feelings are generated at devotional meetings? _____

    _____

5. What is the effect of the spiritually heightened conversations that naturally occur at devotional meetings? _____

    _____

6.	Write a few words about the respectful attitude we should show when praying, whether alone or in a gathering.

_____
_____
_____
_____
_____
_____
_____

SECTION 11

The first unit of this book focused on the habit of reading passages from the Writings every day and pondering their meaning. You have reflected here on the significance of prayer and have, as a result, reinforced the habit of praying daily. The previous section brought to your attention the importance of community worship. All that you have studied so far has prepared you to undertake, if you wish, a first act on the path of service: hosting a devotional meeting.

As an initial step, you may want to memorize several prayers and find an opportunity to share them with a few friends. At the same time, you could ensure that you attend at least one devotional meeting in your community and are counted among its enthusiastic supporters. Eventually, then, you may decide to host a devotional meeting yourself, inviting your friends, family members, and neighbors to gather regularly for prayer and fellowship. It is not uncommon for two or three participants of this course to start such a devotional meeting together.

As you can imagine, there are no formulas for how a devotional meeting is to be organized. But it is clearly a gathering of friends in which prayers are offered, passages from the Writings are read, and uplifting conversations take place—all in a markedly spiritual atmosphere. Can you say a few words about each of the following ideas, in the context of hosting a devotional meeting?

Extending warm and loving invitations: _____

_____
_____
_____

Creating a welcoming environment: _____

_____
_____
_____

Maintaining an atmosphere of reverence: _____

_____

_____

_____

Promoting joyful fellowship: _____

_____

_____

_____

Encouraging spiritually uplifting conversation: _____

_____

_____

_____

REFERENCES

1.   *Gleanings from the Writings of Bahá'u'lláh* (Wilmette: Bahá'í Publishing Trust, 1983, 2017 printing), XLIII, par. 4, p. 105.

2.   Bahá'u'lláh, in *Trustworthiness: A Compilation of Extracts from the Bahá'í Writings*, compiled by the Research Department of the Universal House of Justice (London: Bahá'í Publishing Trust, 1987), no. 21, p. 5.

3.   *The Call of the Divine Beloved: Selected Mystical Works of Bahá'u'lláh* (Haifa: Bahá'í World Centre, 2018), no. 2.43, p. 31.

4.   From a talk given on 5 May 1912, published in *The Promulgation of Universal Peace: Talks Delivered by 'Abdu'l-Bahá during His Visit to the United States and Canada in 1912* (Wilmette: Bahá'í Publishing, 2012), p. 127.

5.   Bahá'u'lláh, *The Hidden Words* (Wilmette: Bahá'í Publishing Trust, 2003, 2012 printing), Arabic no. 13, pp. 6–7.

6.   From a letter dated 8 December 1935 written on behalf of Shoghi Effendi, published in *Prayer and Devotional Life: A Compilation of Extracts from the Writings of Bahá'u'lláh, the Báb, and 'Abdu'l-Bahá and the Letters of Shoghi Effendi and the Universal House of Justice*, compiled by the Research Department of the Universal House of Justice (Wilmette: Bahá'í Publishing, 2019), no. 71, p. 31.

7.   Words of 'Abdu'l-Bahá, cited by J. E. Esslemont, *Bahá'u'lláh and the New Era: An Introduction to the Bahá'í Faith* (Wilmette: Bahá'í Publishing, 2006, 2017 printing), p. 106.

8.   Ibid.

9.   Bahá'u'lláh, in *Bahá'í Prayers: A Selection of Prayers Revealed by Bahá'u'lláh, the Báb, and 'Abdu'l-Bahá* (Wilmette: Bahá'í Publishing Trust, 2002, 2017 printing), pp. 7–8.

10. Ibid., p. 9.

11. Words of 'Abdu'l-Bahá, cited in *Star of the West*, vol. 8, no. 4 (17 May 1917), p. 41.

12. *Gleanings from the Writings of Bahá'u'lláh*, CXXXVI, par. 2, p. 334; also in *Bahá'í Prayers*, p. iii.

13. Bahá'u'lláh, in *Bahá'í Prayers*, pp. 8–9.

14. Ibid., p. 12.

15. 'Abdu'l-Bahá, in *Prayer and Devotional Life*, no. 24, p. 7.

16. From a talk given by 'Abdu'l-Bahá on 5 August 1912, published in *The Promulgation of Universal Peace*, p. 345.

17.   *Selections from the Writings of 'Abdu'l-Bahá* (Wilmette: Bahá'í Publishing, 2010, 2015 printing), no. 22.1, pp. 75–76.

18.   From a letter dated 10 January 1936 written on behalf of Shoghi Effendi, published in *Prayer and Devotional Life*, no. 61, p. 25.

19.   From a letter dated 10 January 1936 written on behalf of Shoghi Effendi, quoted in *Bahá'í Prayers*, p. 301.

20.   Bahá'u'lláh, in *Bahá'í Prayers*, p. 4.

21.   Bahá'u'lláh, in *Prayer and Devotional Life*, no. 68, p. 29.

22.   From a message dated 29 December 2015, published in *Framework for Action: Selected Messages of the Universal House of Justice and Supplementary Material, 2006–2016* (West Palm Beach: Palabra Publications, 2017), no. 35.49, p. 232.

Life and Death

Purpose

To appreciate that life does not consist merely
of the changes and chances of this world
but finds its true significance in
the development of the soul

SECTION 1

The human soul is exalted above matter and the physical world. In one of His talks, 'Abdu'l-Bahá explains:

> "These material bodies are composed of atoms; when these atoms begin to separate decomposition sets in, then comes what we call death. . . .

> "With the soul it is different. The soul is not a combination of elements, it is not composed of many atoms, it is of one indivisible substance and therefore eternal. It is entirely out of the order of the physical creation; it is immortal!"[1]

1. What does "composed of" mean? _____

2. Is the human soul composed of various elements, as are material bodies? _____

3. Is the human soul a physical entity? _____

SECTION 2

A letter written on behalf of the Guardian states that "the soul of man comes into being at conception".[2] Responding to a question about the meaning of "conception", the Universal House of Justice notes:

> "Nothing from the Bahá'í Writings has been found that precisely defines the biological moment and nature of the event described as 'conception'. The use of the term in a medical context also appears to be imprecise. Indeed, one understanding of conception is that it coincides with fertilization; yet another is that it occurs following fertilization and implantation, the onset of pregnancy. Thus, it may not be possible to know when the association of the soul with the material form occurs, and such questions may be insoluble by human thought or investigation since they relate to mysteries of the spiritual world and the nature of the soul itself."[3]

1. When does the human soul come into being? _____
    _____

2. Does the term "conception" describe a precise biological moment? _____

SECTION 3

The connection between the soul and the body is not material; the soul does not enter or leave the body and does not occupy physical space. Its association with the body is similar to that of a light with a mirror which reflects it. The light appearing in the mirror is not inside it. Similarly, the soul is not inside the body. As 'Abdu'l-Bahá indicates, "the rational soul, or the human spirit, does not subsist through this body by inherence—that is to say, it does not enter it; for inherence and entrance are characteristics of bodies, and the rational soul is sanctified above this. It never entered this body to begin with, that it should require, upon leaving it, some other abode. No, the connection of the spirit with the body is even as the connection of this lamp with a mirror. If the mirror is polished and perfected, the light of the lamp appears therein, and if the mirror is broken or covered with dust, the light remains concealed."[4]

1. Fill in the blanks in the sentences below.

    a. The rational soul, or _____ , does not subsist through the body by inherence—that is to say, the soul does not _____ .

    b. The _____ , or the human spirit, does not enter the body; for inherence and entrance are _____ , and the rational soul is _____ .

    c. The soul never _____ to begin with, that it should require, upon leaving it, _____ .

    d. The connection of the spirit with the body is like the connection of a _____ _____ .

    e. If the mirror is polished and perfected, _____ appears in it.

    f. If the mirror is broken or covered with dust, _____ _____ .

2. On the basis of what we have studied up to now, determine whether the following are true:

    _____ The soul does not belong to the physical world.

    _____ The soul is within the body.

    _____ The body is the owner of the soul.

    _____ The soul is immortal.

    _____ The individual has his or her beginning when the soul associates itself with the embryo.

    _____ Life begins when the individual is born into this world.

    _____ The individual's material existence continues after death.

    _____ Life consists of the things that happen to us every day.

3.   Use the image of a light and a mirror to describe the relationship between the soul and the body: _____

_____

_____

_____

_____

SECTION 4

There is a very special relationship between the soul and the body, which together form a human being. This relationship lasts the span of a mortal life only. When the association between them ceases, each one returns to its origin—the body to the world of dust and the soul to the spiritual worlds of God, where it continues to progress. 'Abdu'l-Bahá states:

"The human spirit has a beginning but no end: It endures forever."[5]

In one of His talks, He clarifies:

"The spirit does not need a body, but the body needs spirit, or it cannot live. The soul can live without a body, but the body without a soul dies."[6]

And the Guardian explains:

"With regard to the soul of man: According to the Bahá'í Teachings the human soul starts with the formation of the human embryo, and continues to develop and pass through endless stages of existence after its separation from the body. Its progress is thus infinite."[7]

1.   With the above quotations in mind, answer the following questions:

   a.   Does the body need a soul? _____

   b.   Does the soul need the body? _____

   c.   What happens to the connection between the body and the soul when we die?

   _____

   d.   What happens to the soul after death? _____

   _____

   e.   How long does the progress of the soul last? _____

   _____

   f.   When does life end? _____

   _____

2.	Decide which of the following are in agreement with what we have studied in these sections:

_____ Death is a punishment.

_____ The connection between the body and soul lasts the span of a mortal life only.

_____ The body is capable of eternal progress.

_____ The soul will progress forever.

_____ Death is the end of life.

_____ There will be a day of judgment when our bodies will rise up.

_____ At death, the soul has more freedom than it did before.

_____ Life ends with death.

_____ We should fear death.

_____ Food, clothes, rest, and recreation are necessary for the soul.

_____ The soul becomes tired as the body uses up its energy.

_____ The soul is not affected by illness or by weakness of the body.

_____ The human being will still have physical needs after death.

SECTION 5

We have seen that the soul does not occupy physical space and does not operate according to the laws of nature, as do material entities. The soul exerts influence in the world through the agency of the body, but this is not the only means through which the soul exercises its power. Bahá'u'lláh declares:

> **"Verily I say, the human soul is exalted above all egress and regress. It is still, and yet it soareth; it moveth, and yet it is still."[8]**

And 'Abdu'l-Bahá tells us:

> **"Know that the influence and perception of the human spirit is of two kinds; that is, the human spirit has two modes of operation and understanding. One mode is through the mediation of bodily instruments and organs. Thus it sees with the eye, hears with the ear, speaks with the tongue. . . .**

> **"The other mode of the spirit's influence and action is without these bodily instruments and organs."[9]**

1.	Fill in the blanks in the following sentences:

a.	The human soul is exalted above all _____ and _____ .

b.	It is _____ , and yet it _____ .

c.	It _____ , and yet it is _____ .

2.   Describe the two ways through which the soul perceives and exerts influence in this
     world: _____

     _____

     _____

     _____

3.   Can you give examples of the soul's influence and action without bodily instruments?

     _____

     _____

     _____

     _____

SECTION 6

Now, in light of the discussion in the preceding sections, read the following passage from the Writings of Bahá'u'lláh:

> **"Know thou that the soul of man is exalted above, and is independent of all infirmities of body or mind. That a sick person showeth signs of weakness is due to the hindrances that interpose themselves between his soul and his body, for the soul itself remaineth unaffected by any bodily ailments. Consider the light of the lamp. Though an external object may interfere with its radiance, the light itself continueth to shine with undiminished power. In like manner, every malady afflicting the body of man is an impediment that preventeth the soul from manifesting its inherent might and power. When it leaveth the body, however, it will evince such ascendancy, and reveal such influence as no force on earth can equal. Every pure, every refined and sanctified soul will be endowed with tremendous power, and shall rejoice with exceeding gladness."[10]**

1.   Explain in your own words how the soul remains unaffected by the infirmities of
     body or mind, and what will be made evident upon its separation from the body.

     _____

     _____

     _____

     _____

     _____

     _____

     _____

2.   Will we maintain our individuality after the death of our physical bodies? _____

SECTION 7

Bahá'u'lláh tells us:

> "And now concerning thy question regarding the soul of man and its survival after death. Know thou of a truth that the soul, after its separation from the body, will continue to progress until it attaineth the presence of God, in a state and condition which neither the revolution of ages and centuries, nor the changes and chances of this world, can alter. It will endure as long as the Kingdom of God, His sovereignty, His dominion and power will endure. It will manifest the signs of God and His attributes, and will reveal His loving kindness and bounty."[11]

1. How long will the soul continue to progress after physical death? _____
   _____

2. In what state will the soul continue its eternal journey towards the presence of God?
   _____
   _____
   _____

3. What are some of the attributes and signs the soul will manifest in that state? _____
   _____
   _____

4. On the basis of what we have studied so far, determine whether the following are true:

   _____ The Kingdom of God will last forever.

   _____ The soul has the capacity to manifest the attributes of God.

   _____ The prayers we say for the departed do not affect the progress of their souls.

   _____ The soul never ceases to exist.

SECTION 8

Bahá'u'lláh declares:

> "Know thou that every hearing ear, if kept pure and undefiled, must, at all times and from every direction, hearken to the voice that uttereth these holy words: 'Verily, we are God's, and to Him shall we return.' The mysteries of man's physical death and of his return have not been divulged, and still remain unread. . . .

> "Death proffereth unto every confident believer the cup that is life indeed. It bestoweth joy, and is the bearer of gladness. It conferreth the gift of everlasting life.

"As to those that have tasted of the fruit of man's earthly existence, which is the recognition of the one true God, exalted be His glory, their life hereafter is such as We are unable to describe. The knowledge thereof is with God, alone, the Lord of all worlds."[12]

"O Son of the Supreme! I have made death a messenger of joy to thee. Wherefore dost thou grieve? I made the light to shed on thee its splendor. Why dost thou veil thyself therefrom?"[13]

1.   Which of the following statements are true?

_____ The soul of the human being comes from God and will return to Him.

_____ All knowledge of life after death is with God.

_____ For the confident believer, death is life.

_____ Death is the bearer of gladness.

_____ The mysteries of death are known by all.

_____ We should treasure the bounties of life yet not be afraid of death, for it is a messenger of joy.

_____ It is not important for us to know about life after death.

2.   Now, bearing in mind what we have studied in these sections, write a short paragraph about life, death, body and soul.

_____

_____

_____

_____

_____

_____

_____

_____

_____

_____

_____

_____

_____

SECTION 9

'Abdu'l-Bahá explains:

"In the beginning of his life man was in the world of the womb, wherein he developed the capacity and worthiness to advance to this world. The powers necessary for this world he acquired in that world. He needed eyes in this world; he obtained them in the world of the womb. He needed ears in this world; he obtained them there. All the powers that were needed in this world he acquired in the world of the womb. In that world he became prepared for this world, and when he entered this world he saw that he possessed all the requisite powers and had acquired all the limbs and organs necessary for this life, in that world. It followeth that in this world too he must prepare for the world beyond. That which he needeth in the world of the Kingdom he must obtain and prepare here. Just as he acquired the powers necessary for this world in the world of the womb, so, likewise, he must obtain that which he will need in the world of the Kingdom—that is to say, all the heavenly powers—in this world."[14]

1. Decide whether or not the following are true:

    _____ All the powers necessary for this world are acquired in the world of the womb.

    _____ There is no need to prepare oneself for life in the next world.

    _____ What we need in the world of the Kingdom must be obtained there.

    _____ The purpose of this life is to acquire the powers necessary for life in the next world.

    _____ True life begins when one dies and goes to the divine Kingdom.

    _____ True life begins in this world and continues after physical death.

2. What are some of the capacities the human being receives in the world of the womb?

    _____

    _____

3. What are some of the endowments that should be obtained here for life after death?

    _____

    _____

SECTION 10

Bahá'u'lláh proclaims:

"The whole duty of man in this Day is to attain that share of the flood of grace which God poureth forth for him. Let none, therefore, consider the largeness or smallness of the receptacle. The portion of some might lie in the palm of a man's hand, the portion of others might fill a cup, and of others even a gallon-measure."[15]

1. In light of the above quotation, answer the following questions:

   a. What is the duty of every individual in this Day? _____

   _____

   b. What are some of the blessings you have received from God? _____

   _____

   _____

   c. To what does the word "receptacle" refer in the above quotation? _____

   _____

   d. Why should we not consider "the largeness or smallness" of the capacity with which we have been endowed? _____

   _____

   _____

   _____

   e. What are some of the things that prevent us from receiving our portion of God's grace? _____

   _____

   _____

   _____

2. Which of the following are true?

   _____ The "largeness or smallness" of our capacity refers to how smart we are.

   _____ To serve God, we need to forget our weaknesses and place our whole trust in Him.

   _____ If in this world we do not develop the capacities God has bestowed upon us, our souls will be weak when we arrive in the next world.

SECTION 11

Bahá'u'lláh states:

"Thou hast asked Me concerning the nature of the soul. Know, verily, that the soul is a sign of God, a heavenly gem whose reality the most learned of men hath failed to grasp, and whose mystery no mind, however acute, can ever hope to unravel. It is the first among all created things to declare the excellence of its Creator, the first to recognize His glory, to cleave to His truth, and to bow down in adoration before Him."[16]

1. Fill in the blanks in the following sentences:

   a. The soul is a _____ of God.

   b. The soul is a _____ whose _____ the most learned have failed to grasp, and whose _____ no mind, however acute, can ever hope to _____ .

   c. The soul is the _____ to declare the _____ .

   d. The soul is the first to _____ God's glory.

   e. The soul is the first to _____ God's truth.

   f. The soul is the first to _____ in adoration before God.

2. Which of the following are true?

   _____ "To unravel" means to figure out.

   _____ Among all created things, the first to recognize God is the human brain.

   _____ "Acute" means sharp.

   _____ A learned person understands the mystery of the soul.

   _____ Only great philosophers can declare the excellence of God.

   _____ It is not necessary to think about the soul because we will never be able to understand it.

SECTION 12

Bahá'u'lláh declares:

"Ye are even as the bird which soareth, with the full force of its mighty wings and with complete and joyous confidence, through the immensity of the heavens, until, impelled to satisfy its hunger, it turneth longingly to the water and clay of the earth below it, and, having been entrapped in the mesh of its desire, findeth itself impotent to resume its flight to the realms whence it came. Powerless to shake off the burden weighing on its sullied wings, that bird, hitherto an inmate of the heavens, is now forced to seek a dwelling-place upon the dust. Wherefore, O My servants, defile not your wings with the clay of waywardness and vain desires, and suffer them not to be stained with the dust of envy and hate, that ye may not be hindered from soaring in the heavens of My divine knowledge."[17]

1. Complete the sentences below.

   a. The bird to which Bahá'u'lláh refers in this quotation is the _____ .

b. This bird is an inhabitant of the _____ .

c. If its wings are sullied, the bird is forced to seek its home in the _____ .

2. Now answer the following questions:

a. How do the "wings" of the soul become "sullied"? _____

_____

_____

b. What are some of the burdens that, like "the water and clay of the earth", weigh on the wings of the soul?_____

_____

_____

c. What are some of the things that can prevent us from soaring in the heavens of divine knowledge?_____

_____

_____

d. Why would a soul exchange its heavenly home for the dust of this world? ___

_____

_____

3. Determine whether the following statements are true:

_____ Worldly attachments impede our spiritual progress.

_____ Our waywardness and vain desires hold us back from flying in the heavens of divine knowledge.

_____ Envy and hatred are natural traits of the human being and do not burden the soul.

_____ We can rid ourselves of the burdens that prevent us from soaring through the immensity of the heavens by detaching ourselves from the things of this world.

_____ The soul's home is in this world.

SECTION 13

Bahá'u'lláh says:

"Having created the world and all that liveth and moveth therein, He, through the direct operation of His unconstrained and sovereign Will, chose to confer upon man the unique distinction and capacity to know Him and to love Him—a capacity that must needs be regarded as the generating impulse and the primary

purpose underlying the whole of creation. . . . Upon the inmost reality of each and every created thing He hath shed the light of one of His names, and made it a recipient of the glory of one of His attributes. Upon the reality of man, however, He hath focused the radiance of all of His names and attributes, and made it a mirror of His own Self. Alone of all created things man hath been singled out for so great a favor, so enduring a bounty."[18]

1. Fill in the blanks below.

    a. God chose to confer upon the human being the unique distinction and capacity to _____ .

    b. Upon the inmost reality of _____ and _____ created thing God has shed the light of _____ , and made it a recipient of the glory of _____ .

    c. Upon the reality of the human being, He has focused the radiance of _____ _____ , and made it a mirror of _____ .

2. Now answer the following questions:

    a. Can you mention some of the attributes of God? _____
    _____
    _____

    b. What are some of the attributes of God that the human soul can reflect? _____
    _____
    _____

    c. How can these attributes be manifested? _____
    _____
    _____

    d. For what special favor has the human being been singled out? _____
    _____
    _____

3. Which of the following are true?

    _____ The human being is not distinct from the rest of creation.

    _____ The capacity to know God and to love Him is the generating impulse and the primary purpose underlying the whole of creation.

    _____ The reality of every created thing is the recipient of one of the attributes of God.

    _____ The human soul can reflect all the attributes of God.

SECTION 14

Bahá'u'lláh tells us:

"These energies with which the Daystar of Divine bounty and Source of heavenly guidance hath endowed the reality of man lie, however, latent within him, even as the flame is hidden within the candle and the rays of light are potentially present in the lamp. The radiance of these energies may be obscured by worldly desires even as the light of the sun can be concealed beneath the dust and dross which cover the mirror. Neither the candle nor the lamp can be lighted through their own unaided efforts, nor can it ever be possible for the mirror to free itself from its dross. It is clear and evident that until a fire is kindled the lamp will never be ignited, and unless the dross is blotted out from the face of the mirror it can never represent the image of the sun nor reflect its light and glory."[19]

1. What does the word "latent" mean? _____
    _____

2. What are some of the powers that are latent in the human soul? _____
    _____
    _____

3. What potential does a lamp have? _____

4. What potential does a mirror have? _____

5. What do you have to do to a lamp so that it can give light? _____
    _____

6. What do you have to do to a mirror so that it can reflect light? _____
    _____

7. Can the lamp and the mirror manifest their potential by themselves? _____

8. How can we relate these two examples to the condition of the human soul? ____
    _____
    _____
    _____

9. Who can make the human soul manifest its potential? _____
    _____

SECTION 15

Bahá'u'lláh states:

"The door of the knowledge of the Ancient Being hath ever been, and will continue forever to be, closed in the face of men. No man's understanding shall ever gain access unto His holy court. As a token of His mercy, however, and as a proof of His loving-kindness, He hath manifested unto men the Daystars of His divine guidance, the Symbols of His divine unity, and hath ordained the knowledge of these sanctified Beings to be identical with the knowledge of His own Self. Whoso recognizeth them hath recognized God. Whoso hearkeneth to their call, hath hearkened to the Voice of God, and whoso testifieth to the truth of their Revelation, hath testified to the truth of God Himself. Whoso turneth away from them, hath turned away from God, and whoso disbelieveth in them, hath disbelieved in God. Every one of them is the Way of God that connecteth this world with the realms above, and the Standard of His Truth unto every one in the kingdoms of earth and heaven. They are the Manifestations of God amidst men, the evidences of His Truth, and the signs of His glory."[20]

1. With the above quotation in mind, answer the following questions:

    a. Is it possible for us to know God directly? _____

    b. How, then, can we know God? _____

        _____

    c. Can you name some of the Daystars of divine guidance? _____

        _____

    d. To Whose Voice have those who have listened to the Manifestations of God hearkened? _____

        _____

    e. From Whom are we turning away when we ignore the call of the Manifestations of God? _____

2. Complete the following sentences:

    a. The door of the knowledge of the Ancient Being hath ever been, and will continue forever to be, _____ .

    b. No man's understanding shall ever gain access unto _____ .

    c. God sent His Manifestations as a token of His _____ and as a proof of His _____ .

    d. The knowledge of the Manifestations of God is identical with _____ _____ .

e. Whoso recognizes Them has _____ .

f. Whoso hearkens to Their call has _____ ____ .

g. Every one of Them is the Way of God that _____

_____

_____ .

3. Which of the following are true?

____ We can grow spiritually through our efforts alone.

____ God has given us a mind, and it is sufficient for our progress.

____ We will progress spiritually by recognizing the Manifestation of God and will not have to put forth more effort.

____ We can progress spiritually by recognizing the Manifestation of God and by making effort to live according to His teachings.

____ We can know God directly.

____ The human being can become just like God.

____ God is exalted above human comprehension.

____ When we listen to the words of a Manifestation of God, we are listening to the Voice of God.

SECTION 16

Bahá'u'lláh declares:

"The Prophets and Messengers of God have been sent down for the sole purpose of guiding mankind to the straight Path of Truth. The purpose underlying Their revelation hath been to educate all men, that they may, at the hour of death, ascend, in the utmost purity and sanctity and with absolute detachment, to the throne of the Most High."[21]

And in another passage, He says:

"Man is the supreme Talisman. Lack of a proper education hath, however, deprived him of that which he doth inherently possess. Through a word proceeding out of the mouth of God he was called into being; by one word more he was guided to recognize the Source of his education; by yet another word his station and destiny were safeguarded. The Great Being saith: Regard man as a mine rich in gems of inestimable value. Education can, alone, cause it to reveal its treasures, and enable mankind to benefit therefrom. If any man were to meditate on that which the Scriptures, sent down from the heaven of God's holy Will, have revealed, he would readily recognize that their purpose is that all men shall be regarded as one soul, so that the seal bearing the words 'The Kingdom shall be God's' may be stamped on every heart, and the light of Divine bounty, of grace, and mercy may envelop all mankind."[22]

1. For what purpose have the Prophets and Messengers of God been sent down? ____

    _____

    _____

2. What is the purpose underlying Their revelation? _____

    _____

    _____

    _____

3. What does the word "talisman" mean? _____

    _____

4. What is the consequence of the lack of a proper education? _____

    _____

5. What can a proper education cause? _____

    _____

    _____

6. What is the Source of our education? _____

7. What is our destiny? _____

    _____

8. What are some of the gems education reveals?_____

    _____

9. What do we readily recognize when we meditate on the Holy Writings? _____

    _____

    _____

    _____

    _____

SECTION 17

Bahá'u'lláh states:

"Thou hast, moreover, asked Me concerning the state of the soul after its separation from the body. Know thou, of a truth, that if the soul of man hath walked in the ways of God, it will, assuredly, return and be gathered to the glory of the Beloved. By the righteousness of God! It shall attain a station such as no pen

can depict, or tongue describe. The soul that hath remained faithful to the Cause of God, and stood unwaveringly firm in His Path shall, after his ascension, be possessed of such power that all the worlds which the Almighty hath created can benefit through him."[23]

1.   Complete the following sentences:

a.   If a soul has walked in the ways of God, it will, assuredly, _____

    _____ .

b.   It will attain a station such as _____

    _____ .

c.   The _____ that has remained _____ to the _____ of _____ , and has _____ unwaveringly _____ in _____ _____ shall, after _____ , be possessed of such _____ that all the worlds which the _____ has _____ can _____ through him.

SECTION 18

Bahá'u'lláh tells us:

"Blessed is the soul which, at the hour of its separation from the body, is sanctified from the vain imaginings of the peoples of the world. Such a soul liveth and moveth in accordance with the Will of its Creator, and entereth the all-highest Paradise. The Maids of Heaven, inmates of the loftiest mansions, will circle around it, and the Prophets of God and His chosen ones will seek its companionship. With them that soul will freely converse, and will recount unto them that which it hath been made to endure in the path of God, the Lord of all worlds."[24]

"He should forgive the sinful, and never despise his low estate, for none knoweth what his own end shall be. How often hath a sinner attained, at the hour of death, to the essence of faith, and, quaffing the immortal draught, hath taken his flight unto the Concourse on high! And how often hath a devout believer, at the hour of his soul's ascension, been so changed as to fall into the nethermost fire!"[25]

1.   In what state should our soul be when its separates from the body? _____

    _____

2.   What are some vain imaginings? _____

    _____

    _____

    _____

3. In what condition will a soul sanctified from vain imaginings live and move after death? _____

_____

_____

_____

4. Who will be the companions of such a soul? _____

_____

5. Will such a soul be able to converse with the Prophets of God and His chosen ones?

_____

6. Do we know beforehand how and when our earthly life will end? _____

7. What can we do now to attain the eternal life destined for us? _____

_____

_____

SECTION 19

'Abdu'l-Bahá explains:

"As the spirit of man lives forever after casting off this elemental frame, it is, like all existing things, undoubtedly capable of progress, and thus one may pray for a departed soul to advance, to be forgiven, or to be made the recipient of divine favors, bounties, and grace. That is why, in the prayers of Bahá'u'lláh, the forgiveness and pardon of God are implored for those who have ascended to the next world. Moreover, just as people are in need of God in this world, so too are they in need of Him in the next. The creatures are ever in need, and God is ever completely independent of them, whether in this world or in the world to come."[26]

Why should we pray for the souls of the departed?

_____

_____

_____

_____

_____

_____

_____

_____

SECTION 20

'Abdu'l-Bahá writes:

"When the human soul soareth out of this transient heap of dust and riseth into the world of God, then veils will fall away, and verities will come to light, and all things unknown before will be made clear, and hidden truths be understood.

"Consider how a being, in the world of the womb, was deaf of ear and blind of eye, and mute of tongue; how he was bereft of any perceptions at all. But once, out of that world of darkness, he passed into this world of light, then his eye saw, his ear heard, his tongue spoke. In the same way, once he hath hastened away from this mortal place into the Kingdom of God, then he will be born in the spirit; then the eye of his perception will open, the ear of his soul will hearken, and all the truths of which he was ignorant before will be made plain and clear."[27]

1. Fill in the blanks below.

   a. When the human soul leaves this world, then

      – veils _____,

      – and verities _____,

      – and all things unknown before _____,

      – and hidden truths _____.

   b. In the world of the _____ , we were _____ of ear, _____ of eye, and _____ of tongue.

   c. When we were born into this world, then our eye _____ , our ear _____ , and our tongue _____ .

   d. In the same way, when we pass on to the Kingdom of God, we will be _____ in the _____ .

   e. Then the eye of our _____ will _____ , the ear of our _____ will _____ , and all the _____ of which we were ignorant before will be made _____ and _____ .

2. Decide whether the following statements are true:

   _____ When we are in the world of the womb, we know about this world.

   _____ Our condition after death is a truth hidden to us in this life.

   _____ Horizons, entirely new, will open before us after death.

   _____ When we die, we return to this world to be born again.

SECTION 21

Bahá'u'lláh states:

"And now concerning thy question whether human souls continue to be conscious one of another after their separation from the body. Know thou that the souls of the people of Bahá, who have entered and been established within the Crimson Ark, shall associate and commune intimately one with another, and shall be so closely associated in their lives, their aspirations, their aims and strivings as to be even as one soul. They are indeed the ones who are well-informed, who are keen-sighted, and who are endued with understanding. Thus hath it been decreed by Him Who is the All-Knowing, the All-Wise.

"The people of Bahá, who are the inmates of the Ark of God, are, one and all, well aware of one another's state and condition, and are united in the bonds of intimacy and fellowship. Such a state, however, must depend upon their faith and their conduct. They that are of the same grade and station are fully aware of one another's capacity, character, accomplishments and merits. They that are of a lower grade, however, are incapable of comprehending adequately the station, or of estimating the merits, of those that rank above them. Each shall receive his share from thy Lord. Blessed is the man that hath turned his face towards God, and walked steadfastly in His love, until his soul hath winged its flight unto God, the Sovereign Lord of all, the Most Powerful, the Ever-Forgiving, the All-Merciful."[28]

1. In the next world, will we recognize people we have known in this world? _____

2. How close will the association between souls be in the next world? _____
   _____

3. On what will differences and distinctions among souls in the next world depend?
   _____
   _____

4. Will anyone be deprived of God's grace? _____

SECTION 22

Bahá'u'lláh exhorts us:

"O My servants! Sorrow not if, in these days and on this earthly plane, things contrary to your wishes have been ordained and manifested by God, for days of blissful joy, of heavenly delight, are assuredly in store for you. Worlds, holy and spiritually glorious, will be unveiled to your eyes. You are destined by Him, in this world and hereafter, to partake of their benefits, to share in their joys, and to obtain a portion of their sustaining grace. To each and every one of them you will, no doubt, attain."[29]

1. Decide which of the following are true:

    _____ We should be filled with sorrow when things are not the way we want them to be.

    _____ All, be it good or bad, is ordained by God.

    _____ Days of blissful joy are awaiting all of us.

    _____ We are sure to see worlds that are holy and spiritually glorious.

    _____ It is our destiny to partake of the benefits of worlds that are holy and spiritually glorious, both in this life and in the life hereafter.

2. Why should we not be filled with sorrow when things contrary to our wishes come to pass?_____

    _____

    _____

    _____

3. What promise does Bahá'u'lláh make to us in this passage? _____

    _____

    _____

    _____

SECTION 23

In this unit, you have reflected on the meaning of human life. You have learned a great deal about the nature of the soul, the purpose of life in this world, the imperative of developing spiritual qualities, and the promise given to us of an eternal life, glorious and filled with joy. In the second unit of the book, we spoke of a twofold purpose—to pursue our own spiritual and intellectual growth and to contribute to the transformation of society. Here is an opportunity to return to that concept and think about the significance of attending to both aspects of this purpose, in light of the insights you have gained about the progress of the soul. Your reflections may benefit from a discussion on the themes below in your group.

1. *Developing spiritual qualities*

2. *Obeying the laws of God*

3. *Contributing to the well-being of the human race*

4. *Advancing on the path of service*

REFERENCES

1. From a talk given on 10 November 1911, published in *Paris Talks: Addresses Given by 'Abdu'l-Bahá in 1911* (Wilmette: Bahá'í Publishing, 2006, 2016 printing), no. 29.12–13, p. 109.

2. From a letter dated 1 April 1946 written on behalf of Shoghi Effendi, published in *Lights of Guidance: A Bahá'í Reference File* (New Delhi: Bahá'í Publishing Trust, 1988, 2010 printing), no. 1820, p. 537.

3. From a letter dated 28 July 2016 written on behalf of the Universal House of Justice.

4. 'Abdu'l-Bahá, in *Some Answered Questions* (Wilmette: Bahá'í Publishing, 2014, 2016 printing), no. 66.3, pp. 352–53.

5. Ibid., no. 38.5, p. 220.

6. From a talk given by 'Abdu'l-Bahá on 9 November 1911, published in *Paris Talks*, no. 28.16, p. 104.

7. From a letter dated 31 December 1937 written on behalf of Shoghi Effendi, published in *Lights of Guidance*, no. 680, p. 204.

8. *Gleanings from the Writings of Bahá'u'lláh* (Wilmette: Bahá'í Publishing Trust, 1983, 2017 printing), LXXXII, par. 8, p. 183.

9. 'Abdu'l-Bahá, in *Some Answered Questions*, no. 61.1–2, p. 334.

10. *Gleanings from the Writings of Bahá'u'lláh*, LXXX, par. 2, p. 174.

11. Ibid., LXXXI, par. 1, p. 176.

12. Ibid., CLXV, par. 1–3, pp. 391–92.

13. Bahá'u'lláh, *The Hidden Words* (Wilmette: Bahá'í Publishing Trust, 2003, 2012 printing), Arabic no. 32, p. 11.

14. From a talk given on 6 July 1912, published in *The Promulgation of Universal Peace: Talks Delivered by 'Abdu'l-Bahá during His Visit to the United States and Canada in 1912* (Wilmette: Bahá'í Publishing, 2012), pp. 315–16. (authorized translation)

15. *Gleanings from the Writings of Bahá'u'lláh*, V, par. 4, p. 8.

16. Ibid., LXXXII, par. 1, pp. 179–80.

17. Ibid., CLIII, par. 6, pp. 370–71.

18. Ibid., XXVII, par. 2, pp. 72–73.

19. Ibid., XXVII, par. 3, p. 73.

20.   Ibid., XXI, par. 1, pp. 54–55.

21.   Ibid., LXXXI, par. 1, p. 177.

22.   Ibid., CXXII, par. 1, pp. 293–94.

23.   Ibid., LXXXII, par. 7, p. 182.

24.   Ibid., LXXXI, par. 1, pp. 176–77.

25.   Ibid., CXXV, par. 3, pp. 300–1.

26.   'Abdu'l-Bahá, in *Some Answered Questions*, no. 62.3, pp. 340–41.

27.   *Selections from the Writings of 'Abdu'l-Bahá* (Wilmette: Bahá'í Publishing, 2010, 2015 printing), no. 149.3–4, pp. 246–47.

28.   *Gleanings from the Writings of Bahá'u'lláh*, LXXXVI, par. 1–2, pp. 192–93.

29.   Ibid., CLIII, par. 9, p. 373.